STORY SAILING®
A GUIDE TO STORYTELLING FOR SPEAKERS, TRAINERS, & COACHES

BY DAVE BRICKER

ESSENTIAL ABSURDITIES PRESS

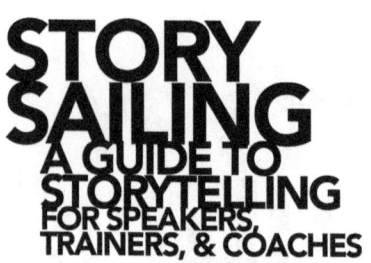

STORY SAILING
A GUIDE TO STORYTELLING FOR SPEAKERS, TRAINERS, & COACHES

BY DAVE BRICKER

©2019, Coral Gables, FL, USA

This book may not be reproduced, transmitted, or stored in whole or in part by any means, including graphic, electronic, or mechanical without the express written consent of the publisher except in the case of brief quotations embodied in critical articles and reviews.

Cover and book design by Dave Bricker.

Edited by Steven Bauer *of* HollowTreeLiterary.com

ISBN: 978-0-9862960-4-8

ESSENTIAL ABSURDITIES PRESS

http://www.storysailing.com

for Eva

Introduction

Savvy speakers know that stories are what elevates a message above the din. Just adding data to the roaring river of bits and bytes won't cut it.

This realization has spawned business buzzphrases like "narrative strategy" and "story consciousness." Columbia University now offers a course called *Strategic Storytelling: Maximum Impact in a Digital World*. Corporate giants like IBM and Verizon have "Chief Storytelling Officers" on staff. A search on LinkedIn reveals over 825,000 people with "storytelling" in their title. Storytelling workshops, seminars, and books are marketed to speakers, salespeople, customer service agents, bloggers, and other professionals who want to connect, engage, influence, persuade, and communicate. Storytelling is *in*.

But if stories are such powerful tools, why are the mysteries of how they work not revealed to us in grade school? How is it that the story about storytelling is among our society's missing narratives?

Storytelling workshop attendees arrive with a common set of conflicts and questions:

> I know a good story when I hear one, but how do effective stories work?
>
> How do I get from "This is what happened" to "Here's my *story?*"
>
> How do I create a narrative that attracts and holds listeners' attention?
>
> I've had a safe, conventional life. How can I find good stories to tell?
>
> I love stories, but I'm not a storyteller. How can I find my story and connect with listeners?
>
> I've had exciting adventures. How do I tell my story in a way that isn't self-celebratory?
>
> I survived tremendous darkness. How do I tell my story without making my audience depressed?
>
> Is it dishonest or unethical to tell a story that isn't entirely true?
>
> How do I place my story in the service of my listeners?

The answers can be found in StorySailing®, an easy-to-understand thought model that explains how stories work. A survey of common storytelling mistakes inspires a better understanding of why some stories connect—and why some don't. In this short guide to storytelling, you'll find the footprints of speakers who could have engaged their audiences more deeply, and of those who will encourage you to use the magic of storytelling to build deep, emotional, and powerful connections that change minds, lives, and fortunes.

StorySailing®

WHEN I WAS A YOUNG MAN still in college, I found myself—quite through happenstance—in the company of an odd band of folks who lived aboard their sailboats in the free anchorage in Miami. The stories they told about adventures in faraway places captivated me. Up until then, I'd been a private prep-school student headed toward some sort of advanced degree and the career that followed, but when I realized that tales of adventure at sea were not just the stuff of books and movies, I resolved to find stories of my own.

The secret floating village of Miami's Dinner Key Anchorage was a storybook Steinbeck himself would have envied. I took notes and photographs and began to develop a "story consciousness"—a sense that stories were everywhere, swirling all around me. I didn't know exactly what stories were or how they worked, but I made it my business to look for them. My first important realization was that, no matter how grandiose the setting or severe the storm, *stories are always about people.* Put colorful people in a colorful setting and give them colorful things to do, and you've got stories to tell. Take away the people and you've got nothing. If a tree falls in the forest and there's no one around to hear, does it make a sound? No.

Not long after graduation, I found myself on a tiny blue sailboat in the middle of the Gulf Stream *en route* to the Bahamas. Over the years, I made several Gulf Stream crossings, spent thirty-eight days transiting the North Atlantic, ran aground more than once, battled storms, speared fish on the reefs, anchored in the lee of tranquil islands, climbed an 8000-foot volcano, met wonderful people, experienced deep solitude, got seasick a few times, and returned home.

But having voyaged in search of stories and found them, I still wasn't sure how stories worked. I knew that stories were about people, but I also knew that stories ran deeper than journalistic accounts of who, what, where, when, why, and how. I worked in a number of disciplines and wrote a number of books before I solved that mystery.

One overarching theme encompasses all of literature and human endeavor—the search for meaning. Meaning is, itself, one of the Essential Absurdities; no one can say what "meaning" means, but we can postulate that meaningfulness has to do with the degree to which something resonates with our passions, personality, or purpose; or with our innate will to survive and procreate. What stories do — as opposed to other kinds of information like prices, processes, ingredients, and data — is communicate meaning from one person to another. Stories are connecting tools.

A story is a metaphorical boat that sails from the rocky, stormy seas of *conflict* to the safe port of *transformation*. Whether it's Cinderella finding "happily ever after" or a business coach challenging her clients to understand their value and charge what they're worth, the *story* is about the outcome — the *transformation.*

For the story to engage — for the boat to make the passage — the water has to be "deep" enough; the conflict has to be *authentic.* Whatever boat you choose must be a way to tell not just your story but your listener's story as well. We care about Cinderella because we all want to find our prince or princess. We all want to be loved for the subtle, nearly invisible things that make us who we are — our "walk" — that glass slipper that fits only us. The Cinderella story is authentic, even if it isn't true or plausible.

To make the crossing, the sailboat needs wind — an invisible, powerful force — *magic.* Cinderella had her fairy godmother, but perhaps you're a business speaker who can transform the culture of an organization in forty-five minutes. Do you teach autistic children to speak or shoot photographs that transport viewers to other worlds? Do you invent drugs that save lives or play music that makes people dance? Are you great at math or chemistry? Do you make wine or cook transcendent meals or show people how to climb mountains? Magic is no more confined to the realm of books and movies than adventure is

A story is a ship full of *people,* pushed from the stormy seas of *conflict* through the deep waters of *authenticity* by the winds of *magic,* to a safe port of *transformation.* Use this model to see more deeply into the narratives you craft and encounter. Studying the art of storytelling will empower you to be the magic wind that blows your audience from conflict to transformation. This is StorySailing.

MAGIC
the invisible force that moves your story forward
(wind) (perspective) (awareness)

storms — *resolution*

CONFLICT → **TRANSFORMATION**

rocks — *safe harbor*

is the story (or the water) deep enough to keep the ship afloat?
is the story a metaphor for the listener's story?
AUTHENTICITY

Storytelling Styles

A PEEK AT COMMON STORYTELLING STYLES through the StorySailing lens reveals why so many presenters fail to engage, inspire, and educate listeners—and why a few establish themselves as experts, leaders, agents of change, and visionaries.

Transformation

> In 1991, I sailed from the Bahamas to the Azores. Fifteen years later, I returned with my family on an airliner, toured this peaceful and beautiful volcanic wonderland, and celebrated my daughter's first birthday.

An anecdote recounts a series of factual events. Though the above passage contains characters, an event of personal significance, and an intriguing setting, it depicts no personal redemption, realization, or rebirth. The narrative provokes no action or actualization in the reader—no journey from conflict to transformation. It's journalism, not storytelling. At best, it might provoke a reader to research the Azores.

We are driven by our search for meaning. When we find none in the messages we're exposed to, we lose focus and return to "survival mode"—scanning the world for threats and opportunities. Speakers and writers who offer anecdotes instead of authentic, *transformational* stories will lose their listeners' attention.

Do you remember where I sailed from or to? Probably not.

Conflict

> As the sun rises, so does Faial's mist. Her gray skirt ascends slowly, climbing the coast toward the middle of the island. Hues of silver and gray soak up color from the new day, revealing verdant, terraced farms. Pastures latticed with lava rock walls rise in a tapestry of green. Church spires punctuate white, red-roofed villages along the coast. The shore is steep—strewn with dark, volcanic rocks. Headlights move on a coastal road. The island is *beautiful*—timeless, provincial, and charming.

Many colorful, well-crafted narratives fail to engage because they introduce no *conflict*. Without environmental and internal obstacles to overcome, the reader is not part of any meaningful *journey*.

The narrative above delivers an experience, but it offers no accounts of the storms, navigational challenges, or long weeks at sea that lay between departure and destination. This is a vignette, not a story—the spice, not the soup.

Part of the magic of stories is that when they're told well, *we experience them as if we were in them.* Though details of characters, settings, and circumstances heighten our sense of *being there,* it is the emotional journey that captivates. Through stories, we are able to fight wars, explore space, suffer deep tragedy and personal loss, travel to fantastic worlds, and embark on inspiring personal journeys from the safety and comfort of an auditorium seat or reading chair. In doing so, we experience fear, sadness, anticipation, excitement, and joy—emotional responses to stimuli we are only vicariously exposed to.

Just as reading the ending first spoils a book, a story without conflict is a short and uninteresting jump to "happily ever after" that will disappoint your listeners. Without conflict there is no reason to embark on a journey. Without a journey, there is no story.

Authenticity

A dynamic and experienced speaker related his experiences traveling to California, hiking among giant redwood trees in the Muir Woods, and fulfilling his dream of crossing the Golden Gate Bridge. He made eye contact with the audience. His timing and tone were dramatic. His body language conveyed the challenges of hiking wooded trails and the difficulty of pushing a baby stroller up the steep streets of San Francisco. "If you've never been to the American west coast," he suggested, "put this trip on your bucket list."

The vivid imagery portrayed by the speaker was engaging; nobody's attention drifted. The story offered conflicts—struggles on the trail, the challenges of traveling with a young family, and a journey to the transformational moment when his dream of crossing the Golden Gate Bridge was fulfilled. And yet, the presentation lacked a certain hard-to-identify *something*.

That missing element was *authentic* conflict. The speaker's personal, individual conflicts of struggling in the woods and wanting to cross the Golden Gate Bridge could have been tied to larger, more universal themes. We all have metaphorical bridges to cross. We all have steep trails to climb. Many of us are uncomfortable confronting nature. Instead of urging us to "Put San Francisco on our bucket list," the speaker could have made *his* story *our* story.

Storytelling Styles | 13

A story is there to transform the listener, not to provide a journalistic account of events. Listeners care about safety, speed, status, sex, food, love, and shelter—matters concerning survival of themselves and the species—and not about whether or not they should visit San Francisco. Had the speaker's journey been symbolic of his listeners' life journeys, the presentation would have been more compelling. A quick reframing of this same story could have positioned it to transform listeners:

> "What are your goals? Your dreams? What bridges must you cross to achieve them? Why don't we all just go out and cross those bridges? Because the big bridge always seems to lie at the far end of a steep and winding road through the dark forest ... and if there isn't a troll hiding under the bridge waiting to eat you, there's a toll booth waiting at the entrance."

This simple set-up would have turned a personal *me*-story about the speaker's vacation into a *you*-story about his listeners' lives. Not only do mythic, archetypal elements like bridges, forests, and mountain paths offer excellent catalysts for story-connection, they are the subconscious drivers of the speaker's own original, powerful experience. Whether he was aware of it or not, the speaker's adventures in the woods and on the bridge were *meaningful* because they tapped into these same universal themes.

Extraordinary events, places, and people make excellent storytelling *elements,* but they are not the story. Dig for deeper, universal meanings — what made the story powerful for *you* — and you'll discover what will make it powerful for your listeners.

Don't Let the Truth Stand in the Way of a Good Story

Rowing up the harbour to make a mail run to the Man-O-War post office, I pass Bill on *Voyager* reading a Bible in his cockpit.

"Mornin', Dave," he calls and waves. "Welcome back. Did you have a good crossing?"

"Thanks," I reply, pulling alongside. "Magic! The Azores were straight out of a fairy tale and with the exception of a few rough days, we had light weather."

Bill, retired on his twenty-eight-foot sloop, lives like a king off a fishing spear and a Social Security check. He keeps to the shade of his cockpit awning. As the morning's low sun paints a bright triangle of light across his cockpit, he adjusts a towel over his bare legs. We chat about my Atlantic crossing for a few minutes before I change the subject on him. "I hope you don't mind me asking, but what's with the Bible? You're the last person I figured…."

"Oh, this?" Bill laughs through his beard. "I'm no holy roller; I'm not even religious. Much of it sounds far-fetched, I admit. A few passages seem to go on forever but the Bible is loaded with stories of struggle, romance, and adventure. People have fought over it for thousands of years; it has a rich history. If nothing else, the Good Book is a pivotal piece of who we are as a society."

"I tried to read it a few times," I confess, "but I never got past Genesis."

Bill smiles. "It's a long crossing. I've been chipping away at it for years, but like life, it has lessons and surprises to offer if you don't take it too seriously ... or experience some powerful epiphany and run around telling the rest of the world what it 'really' means." He winks at me, grins, and raises a silver eyebrow.

Bill and his boat are plausible but fictitious; the encounter described above never happened. Stories are about *people,* and my narrative was better served to have *someone* welcome me back to the Bahamas after my long journey. The truth—that I flew back to the Bahamas, caught the ferry to Man-O-War, returned to my anchored boat without anyone noticing, stowed my gear, and went to sleep—is neither interesting not inspiring. Instead, I used "Bill's Bible" to transition from my return to the Bahamas to a series of new sailing adventures.

The unexpected revelation at the end of the story is another piece of fictitious-but-inspiring storytelling based on true experiences. Not only does it connect the reader to the spiritual experience—the metaphorical "Bible"—of sailing in these islands, it provides a "bookend" or "callback" that brings the story full-circle. After describing visits to a series of islands, the story concludes with the following account of a visitor's impression of the setting:

> Karen beams. In a few days, we've traveled from Marsh Harbour to Little Harbour to Junk Beach, through Whale Cay Passage to Green Turtle Cay, passing places like Man-O-War and Guana Cay that are already part of her collection of cherished memories. "You know," she says. "This world is impossible to describe to someone who hasn't seen it in person."
>
> I smile back at her. "Much of it sounds far-fetched. A few passages seem to go on forever, but life here is loaded with stories of struggle, romance, and adventure. If nothing else, once you experience these islands, they become a pivotal piece of who you are."

Journalists and biographers are well-advised to stick to the facts, but life rarely unfolds in neat and orderly paragraphs and chapters. The storyteller's job is to transform the audience, and for this task, the *essential* truth is sometimes a better tool than the *literal* truth. Narratives that serve the audience are more powerful than narratives that preserve history. Don't let the truth stand in the way of a good story.

Written or Spoken?

I can hear my friend, Kelly Swanson, the master storyteller, calling me out on some of my examples. "You're pulling stuff out of your books, Dave. Some of this sounds like writing, not speaking!"

My passages illustrate my points, but she's right. "Bill's Bible" is probably better consumed from the page than the stage. Though this book is more about story structure than story execution (and it is, after all, a book), consider that spoken language is less formal and more stream-of-consciousness than written prose. Your authentic speaking voice may be quite different from your authentic writing voice. To connect more deeply, make sure your listeners feel talked-to, not read-to.

If I Can Do It, You Can Do It

Is your story about your extraordinary personal journey? Talking about yourself for your own sake will be perceived by listeners as narcissism or an attempt at seeking validation. Stories of dramatic personal transformation can be inspiring and life-changing, but too many storytellers fall into the "If I Can Do it, You Can Do it" trap. Tell your transformational journey story, but do so in a way that positions you as the guide in your listener's story, not as the hero in your own.

> What's keeping you from achieving your dreams?
>
> When I was twenty-three-years old and still in college, I bought my first sailboat for $3000 and began to fix her up with money I made working after school. I knew little about sailing, but I learned the basics by exploring Miami's Biscayne Bay.
>
> A year later, when I sailed across the Gulf Stream to the Bahamas, I had $30 with me, but I was determined to visit the islands I'd heard such marvelous stories about. I odd-jobbed my way around for the next six months, returned to the US, and then went back to the islands on the same miniscule budget.
>
> Eight months later, I joined a friend on a crossing to Gibraltar. I arrived on the other side of the Atlantic without a penny in my pocket, but found work playing music in bars and designing graphics for a small advertising agency.
>
> I made enough money to pay for my passage home, returned to my boat in the Bahamas, and sailed some more.
>
> During this time, I always had food and shelter…

And here comes the curveball:

> If a 24-year-old kid with no money can go out and travel the world, what's holding you back? Maybe it's *you* holding *yourself* back. Maybe your attachment to material things ... blah-blah-blah.

A weak speaker prescribes advice; a strong speaker leads listeners to discover their own truth. "If I Can Do it, You Can Do it" stories are a flawed attempt to shame the audience into imitating you. What kind of leadership is *that?* You may or may not enjoy hearing about my low-budget globe-trotting adventures, but a moralistic and condescending narrative won't help listeners identify or face fears or overcome limiting beliefs.

Numerous speakers and authors share "adversity journey" stories about how they overcame addiction, suffered through paralyzing or disfiguring accidents, endured harsh natural environments, or triumphed after staggering setbacks. Some tell stories of personal achievement—winning Olympic medals and climbing mountains. These stories are seductive because they contain all four elements of engagement—a journey from conflict to transformation through waters deep (authentic) enough to keep the boat off the bottom, usually motivated by the magic wind of determination.

One-legged marathon runners and cancer survivors and climbers of Mount Everest *should* tell their stories, but framing is critical. If listeners conclude, *I could never do that,* your story will backfire.

Be relatable. "I know what you're thinking," is a simple-but-effective storytelling device that switches the focus of the narrative from "I" to "You."

> I know what you're thinking: "Do I have to sail across an ocean or sleep in a volcano to learn how to tell effective stories? Do I need to run a marathon or spend time in a wheelchair or climb Mount Everest?"
>
> Of course not!
>
> What's your ocean? What's your marathon? What's your mountain? We all have challenges and goals....

The authentic message lies not in the story that your fears were faced and your challenges met, but in the story of where and how you found strength, inspiration, courage, or an unlikely solution. Your listener has their *own* set of obstacles to overcome and goals to achieve. They are probably not going to confront adversity or face formidable challenges just because you did (and the results might be disastrous if they tried). Your success is not equal to theirs. What made you decide not to give up that your listener can draw strength from? What inspired you? Did you find a teacher? Did you leverage skills and knowledge you didn't think would be applicable? Did you have a sudden burst of inspiration?

> Global speaker Neal Petersen tells the story of how, as a young black man growing up in apartheid South Africa, he dreamed of racing a sailboat solo around the world — a goal he eventually achieved. "They wouldn't even let me into the yacht club," he tells his audiences. "And I realized I'd have to work for *decades* before I could afford to buy a boat." He pauses to give the audience a moment to feel the conflict. "But though we were poor, my mother was a teacher who always encouraged me to read and learn. I went to the public library and read everything I could about boats and sailing. If I couldn't buy a boat, I'd build my own."

The title of Neal's speech is *No Barriers: Only Solutions*. He does not encourage his listener to build a boat; he encourages them to use available resources to find alternatives, move forward, and achieve their dreams.

As a storyteller, your job is to be the *wind* in your *listeners'* sails — the invisible force that propels *them* from *their* stormy sea of conflict to *their* safe port of transformation. Instead of bragging about your journey, address fundamental limiting thoughts like the conflation of fear with weakness. Bravery is not fearlessness. The most courageous journeys are undertaken by those who allow themselves to feel scared.

> "Was I scared?
> "Of course I was scared! I was a young man living alone in a foreign country, getting ready to sail across an ocean on a wooden boat! If I wasn't scared, I wouldn't be here to tell you this story. Being scared is what keeps us alive."

Can you shift your listeners' perspectives or inspire them to challenge their limiting beliefs? The transference of fear from one set of consequences to another can motivate anyone to accomplish anything.

> "… but I was more afraid of growing old and looking back and regretting all the things I hadn't done because I had been too afraid to do them."

Offer inspiration, not advice. Be a leader, not an animated statue erected in your own honor. Your underlying story doesn't have to change, but it will be more powerful and useful when placed in the service of your listener.

Unfinished Symphonies

> "I want to go back, Dave. This stinks! We're out here in a storm, miles from shore—and now we're taking on water."

Ray points his flashlight into the cabin where fruits and vegetables dislodged from their fishnet storage hammocks tumble around in the water lapping over the floorboards.

I'm still queasy, but I summon up my strength. I speak calmly and put a hand on his shoulder. "Ray, it's three in the morning. We're eight hours out; we can't be very far from West End. We're definitely a lot closer to the Bahamas than we are to Florida. Heading back would be a long, uncomfortable trip; the current will set us far north of Miami. But there's no reason to assume we're off-course and the wind is behind us now. Let's push on."

As we talk, the rain and wind subside; the squall is moving past us.

"I'll pump the bilge and find where the water is coming in, Ray. Try to bail out the dinghy while we have a break in the weather."

When you're afraid in the middle of the ocean, you can't call for help. You can't pay to get off. Once you've boarded the roller coaster, you can't stop the ride no matter how terrified you are. At some point, after all options are exhausted, practicality trumps the panic instinct. You get your head together and focus on making the best of a bad situation.

What storms do you face in life and business? What do you do when the winds and seas grow fierce? Do you panic? Do you abandon ship? Do you scream at the crew? Do you...?

The above narrative leads from the *conflict* of a storm at sea to the *transformation*—the conclusions stated about pressing on despite the fear. Its message is *authentic:* Cool heads prevail in storms at sea—and also in tempests of business and personal communication. The nautical metaphor—the unique wrapper for the message—is part of the unique *magic* I bring to my presentations that differentiates me from speakers who use mountain-climbing or fishing for giant tuna or the interactions of a cast of small-town characters to make their points.

And though the conflict is terrifying, listeners do learn that "the rain and wind subside; the squall is moving past us." Nobody is left stuck "in the pit of despair."

So what's missing? The story is simply unfinished. How many times have you watched a stupid movie or read a boring book all the way through because you had to find out how it ended? People who hear me tell this story will know I survived, but they want to know how we found the leak, bailed the boat out, continued on, and reached our destination. After I tie my leaky-boat-at-sea conflict to their business challenges, I need to finish the story.

> We're no longer sinking. Slowly, slowly, the eastern sky lightens. Waves turn from turgid black to oily gray to cobalt blue. We're still offshore in big, deep water, but I can see the radio tower at West End. Flying fish scatter from our

bow. Casuarina pines on Grand Bahama Island rise from the sea ahead of us. Only a few more miles to go.

"Pit of Despair" Stories

I watched Jannie Kruse give a short talk on "labels." She talked about the categories we put ourselves in—how we label ourselves based on our upbringing, and about her stern and abusive grandfather. To make her point, she stuck a series of "Hello, My Name is..." labels to her blouse upon which were written the words: "Victim," "Powerless," "Weak," and "Worthless."

Her speech was personal and vulnerable. She took the audience to a dark place. We felt the pain of not being valued, and she kept us there for an awkward and powerful moment.

Stories transport listeners into *our* experiences. Audiences feel our feelings, share our reactions, and may even show physiological responses to the places we take them. (Once, when I told a story about a storm at sea, a woman in the audience began to show signs of seasickness.) Taking people into "the pit of despair" can be powerful and effective, but the dark side of the power of story must be handled with care. Had the speaker stopped there, her audience would have spent the rest of the day feeling depressed and worrying about her mental health. Such are the after-effects of this particularly unpleasant type of "unfinished symphony" story. If you drive your listeners into darkness, lead them back to the light.

> After her well-timed pause, Jannie began to talk about the power we have to choose, "Who am I?" One by one, she peeled off the negative labels, stuck them together, and crumpled them into a ball.
>
> She began to create new stickers: "Super Mom," "Inspiration," and "Creator." As she did the "work" to write each new label, she stuck them on her blouse where the old ones had been. This was not a speech about victimhood; it was a message about self-determination and self-love — a story of emotional transformation that was made all the more engaging by a journey from the pit of despair to the mountain top.

StorySailing: Combine the Four Elements of Story

Fifteen years after my original voyage, I wait with my wife and baby daughter in an airport security line. *Will they love these islands as much as I had loved them so many years ago? Will this place still hold the same charm? Will I rediscover this land like I might a lost lover, or find that one or both of us have moved on?*

In 1991, I sailed twenty-six days non-stop to the Azores. I knew nothing of those islands except that they offered a resting stop along my route to Gibraltar. The archipelago's rugged contours on my paper navigation chart suggested a desolate and formidable place.

But on the evening of my twenty-fifth day at sea, the terrestrial smells of cows and grass beckoned. The following morning, as the sun purpled the sky, a skirt of fog rose slowly to reveal a green and mountainous land covered with a lattice of farming terraces, its coast dotted with red-roofed Mediterranean villages.

We pulled into the Horta Marina and tied our ship to concrete docks festooned with colorful paintings left by the hundreds of passage-makers who had landed here before us.

Thus began six unanticipated weeks in paradise. Here in these remote islands, I had never felt so at-home and at-peace. I drank hot mineral water from natural springs; climbed an 8000-foot volcano; and hitchhiked through winding, flower-lined mountain roads that presented a marvelous view of neighboring islands rising from the blue Atlantic.

After staying weeks longer than planned, we departed for Gibraltar late in the season. We battled winter gales and rough seas we would have missed had we not been so enchanted with the Azores—but this was a small price to pay. I knew I would return some day to this place that had so captured my soul.

2006: I am no longer that young vagabond who once harnessed the four winds. I hire a taxi to carry me to a hotel instead of thumbing a ride back to the marina. My fresh fish, supplied by restaurants, is served with Portuguese *Casal Garcia* wine.

Our guide drives us through charming coastal villages with cobblestoned streets, down winding roads lined with purple and white Hortensia flowers, and up into the mountains where volcanic lakes, verdant farms, lava rock houses, and stands of tall cedars overlook the sea.

Suzanne smiles. She feels it, too — an essence — an unnamable magic.

The remnants of my dock painting in the Horta Marina are hardly visible, but I can make out the faded shape of the scrimshawed whale's tooth illustration that commemorated my earlier journey. I close my eyes and inhale slowly, then dip my brush and begin to paint.

I am home.

When we revisit the characters and settings associated with past events, we worry that time and distance might have erased the magic.

Will return journeys to old friends and familiar places disappoint us?

Will we be able to share meaningful stories of the people and places that defined us with our new friends and loved ones?

Are we, ourselves, still meaningful, or are we but living scrapbooks full of faded memories?

My goal is not to get my listener to sail across the ocean or visit the Azores or be like me. The need to take an exotic vacation is not an *authentic conflict*. This story uses my sailing voyage as a vehicle for the exploration of themes any listener can relate to.

The *transformation:* Not only did my family experience the beauty and connection that characterized my original voyage, but I was also able to restore and renew my faded dock painting—a *transformation* of an old memory into a fresh and inspiring new experience that also hints at an eventual return to repeat the process. Revisiting *your* life's most meaningful moments can bring power and color to the present. If you were inspired to think about renewing old memories or friendships, *that's* transformation through storytelling.

Go Beyond the Data

Marketing wisdom tells us to "sell the benefits, not the features." Ignorance of this advice results in mind-numbing, soul-sucking presentations.

> WordPress is a content-management platform used to drive over seventy-five-million websites. Written with open-source technologies like PHP and MySQL, this free software is supported by a huge developer community that extends its functionality through thousands of free and commercial plugins. The aesthetics of WordPress sites are

controlled by an endless selection of "themes"—templates that can be installed with a click.

Asleep yet? This technobabble might be understood by people who already know what WordPress is (and who therefore won't benefit from the presentation), but as a "data dump," it fails to deliver *meaningful* information. Instead of explaining what WordPress does, this speaker would better serve an audience by explaining how WordPress will help them on their own content-sharing, storytelling journeys.

> Imagine being able to create your own web content without having to write code.
>
> Over seventy-five-million web publishers have embraced a free technology called WordPress.
>
> A massive selection of add-ons known as "plugins" empowers you to add almost any functionality you can think of to your website. Want a shopping cart, an e-newsletter with a mailing list subscription form, a booking calendar, or an animated slide show on your website? Plugins allow you to accomplish anything short of scratch-and-sniff.
>
> And when it comes to design, you can choose from thousands of WordPress "themes" that instantly change the look and feel of your message. Many allow you to customize colors, fonts and other design elements with an easy-to-use graphic interface.
>
> Share your message without battling technology. Give WordPress a try.

The rewrite isn't about technology; it's about *people* who have a *conflict*: They want to tell their stories, but they see technology as an intimidating obstacle. They don't care about scripting languages or database technologies. They don't care about the developer community. They'll pay attention when they see that the presentation offers a solution to their problems. And to ensure they do pay attention, the conflict is stated in the opening line.

Data without context is not meaningful. Understand your listener's story. Present your information as a tool they can use to journey from conflict to transformation.

Stories Not Told

"He's got to be a motivational speaker," said Walter. "The NSA holds a big convention every year. This is the National Speakers Association—the NSA that talks, not the NSA that listens. Some of the best speakers in the world attend, and so do a lot of up-and-coming newbies—which is all well and good. This convention is an absolute freak show. It's full of brilliant and talented artists, scientists, thinkers, teachers, trainers, entrepreneurs, masters of inspirational hot air, narcissists, egomaniacs, and some of the most amazing and wonderful people you could ever meet. 'Finding your story' is a big theme within NSA, especially for new speakers who feel called to the platform but don't neces-

> sarily have any idea what to speak about. You can have an absolutely outrageous story and then find the person you're seated next to at dinner was born with no arms or legs, got burned in a fire, was wrongfully imprisoned for a crime he didn't commit, went blind, and then climbed Mt. Everest naked with his upper lip before spending seventy-two days in a life raft. He'll sell you his international bestselling book, too. *Someone* at NSA will have you beat by a mile. Like I said, it's a freak show. I have a good friend in the speaking business who's in a wheelchair because of a plane crash. The joke he hears over and over—and it's told as friendly sarcasm; people are not being insensitive—is that he's *lucky* to have had his story find him. Everyone else has to figure out their stories and speaking topics on their own.

This passage from *The Story Story* describes a common speaker's dilemma. Too many meaningful stories go untold because we fear they're not big enough.

Why should you tell tales about life as a middle manager in a corporate cubicle farm when that other speaker talks about growing his startup company and taking it public?

Why should you talk about raising two children when your best friend has raised five and that other speaker builds orphanages?

Why should I tell my story about sailing across the Atlantic with a friend when Neal Petersen speaks about sailing around the world alone?

The answer is simple: A humble story, well-told, holds more power to change hearts and minds than an epic odyssey that values the storyteller over the listener. Stories and lessons are found as readily in the foothills as on the mountaintop.

Who are *you* to tell the story? A thinker, a feeler, an observer of life—a storyteller with an idea to share. Size doesn't matter.

StorySailing: Craft a Stronger Story

A story is analogous to a boat at sea in a storm. If those aboard are to reach the shelter of a safe harbor, they must steer, trim the sails, stand watches, and take action in spite of their fears. The stormy seas—the challenges faced by those called to action—represent the *conflicts* faced by the story's main character(s). The safe port represents *transformation*, resolution, or redemption. To make the journey successfully, the vessel must sail in water that's sufficiently "deep"; the narrative must touch on an *authentic* and meaningful theme. The fourth story element is *magic*—wind—insight—inspiration—the powerful, invisible force that fills the hero's sails and advances the journey.

Narratives that deliver neither *conflict* nor *transformation* are easy to diagnose. Without a journey, there is no story; without a story, there is no connection.

Narratives that lack *authenticity* may include engaging anecdotes, but they fail to touch on meaningful, universal human themes that connect the listener to the storyteller. Look for this problem when a story sounds good but doesn't quite feel "deep" enough.

Stories that lack *magic* often appear complete; listeners may feel inspired or empowered—but if the storyteller fails to provide a motivating force that blows the listener from fall to redemption, the uplifting effects of the narrative will be short-lived.

Narratives without people in them are "data dumps." Information has no value until a storyteller makes it meaningful to a human listener.

Put your unique talents, skills, experiences, and perspectives—your *magic*—to work for others by telling stories. Instead of being the hero, use your heroic deeds and unique perspectives to inspire listeners to accept your guidance. Instead of carrying them with you on your journey, be the wind that blows them toward transformation on *their* journeys. Mastering the transformation from hero to guide is an authentic journey that storytellers must undertake if they are to engage and transform others. Inspiring your listeners to discover their own magic will embolden them to undertake meaningful voyages of their own.

Resources for Storytellers

I F YOU'RE A PROFESSIONAL SPEAKER or aspire to become one, join the **National Speakers Association.** This community of story-obsessed experts, thought-leaders, and influencers is more than just a professional association. Get involved and offer what value you can. In exchange, you'll find mentorship, encouragement, and clever people to exchange ideas with.

—www.NSASpeakers.com

Toastmasters International has 345,000 members worldwide. Find a chapter near you. Toastmasters speeches typically run between five and seven-and-a-half minutes. Craft your stories, pare them down, share them with a supportive Toastmasters audience, and get the feedback you need. If you're new to speaking, Toastmasters will help you master your natural stage fright and learn to use vocal variety, body language, and other skills of engaging storytellers. If you're an advanced speaker, think of Toastmasters as your "speaking gym." Experiment with new material in front of audiences who aren't paying you to be polished, and learn by mentoring others.

—www.Toastmasters.com

Attend a workshop or keynote by **Kelly Swanson.** Her natural gift for "unpacking" stories, fixing problems, suggesting polishing points, and delivering story *transformation* has been of great value to countless speakers and professionals, including me. Special thanks to Kelly for suggesting, "I know what you're thinking…."

— www.MotivationalSpeakerKellySwanson.com

Allison Shapira's *Speak with Impact* is the best overall reference I've found on speaking and presenting. Though the printed version offers convenience when looking up specific topics, the audiobook version is narrated by Allison, who is, as one would expect, an inspiring speaker.

—www.AllisonShapira.com

Bruce Turkel is a branding expert and National Speakers Association Hall of Fame presenter. Branding is a dialect of storytelling subject to many of the rules and structures discussed in this book. Bruce's book, *All About Them,* offers useful insights on turning *me* stories into *you* stories. If you don't have time to read it, use its title as your mantra.

—www.BruceTurkel.com

Dedication

THE WONDERFUL PEOPLE who have accompanied me on my ongoing speaking and storytelling journey are too numerous to mention, but two deserve special recognition:

I offer my deepest gratitude to Caroline de Posada and Doctor Margarita Gurri for your selfless and tireless encouragement, inspiration, and friendship.

Because independent writers and publishers should be held to the same high standards as the mainstream publishing industry, I encourage you to post an honest and objective review of this book on Amazon.com or the online bookstore of your choice.

Thank you,

— Dave Bricker

Other Books by Dave Bricker

The Dance: a Novel

Waves: a Novel

Currents: a Novel

The One-Hour Guide to Self-Publishing: Straight Talk for Fiction and Nonfiction Writers About Producing and Marketing Your Own Books (out of print)

The Writer's Guide to Powerful Prose

The Blue Monk: A Memoir

The Story Story: A Voyage Through the Islands of Connection and Engagement for Writers, Speakers, Professionals, and Visionaries

The Publisher's Guide to Book Anatomy

Death of the Guitar: Collected Stories, Poems, & Sketches

More StorySailing

WORKING ON A PRESENTATION, speech, article, or book? Read and subscribe to the StorySailing blog; engage Dave Bricker for a keynote or workshop on business writing, storytelling, presentation graphics, or publishing; and get support for your story at www.storysailing.com.

www.ingramcontent.com/pod-product-compliance
Lightning Source LLC
Chambersburg PA
CBHW022344040426
42449CB00006B/719